Introduction

Handwriting Cursive

This *Basics First* book has been carefully designed to help children learn and practice cursive writing. Once children have mastered manuscript writing, they are often eager to learn the cursive style. The activities in this book will help make the transition to cursive writing easy and fun.

This book introduces children to all 26 letters of the alphabet and provides practice in writing letters, words, and sentences. Models are provided so that as children practice, they will be able to correctly write the letter forms.

Letters are introduced according to their strokes, not according to their position in the alphabet. For example, *a* and *d* are presented together because they are formed in a similar manner. As children repeat a series of strokes over and over again, they will gain competence and confidence in their handwriting abilities.

The pages in this book have been arranged so that the words presented for handwriting practice are comprised only of the letters that have already been introduced to the child. Lowercase letters are presented first, followed by capitals. A review of all the letters is provided after each section.

An extension activity accompanies each page. This activity encourages children to think creatively and invites them to use their handwriting skills in a fun and challenging way.

a and d

Name _____

a a a a a

aa aa

d d d d d

dd dd

a   a

add add

dad dad

Try This! Write a sentence about a dad who likes to add.

u and w

Name _____

u *u* *u* *u*

uuu *uuu*

w *w* *w* *w*

ww *ww*

u *u*

out *out*

wet *wet*

Try This! Write a sentence that contains **u** and **w**.
Circle every **u** and **w** you see.

r and s

Name _____

rose

star

Try This! Write three words that contain both **r** and **s**.

m and n

Name _____

m m m m

mm mm

n n n n

nn nn

m   m

mice mice

nine nine

Try This! Write a word that has more than one **m**. Write a word that has more than one **n**.

v and x

Name _____

v

vv

x

xx

v

vet

extra

Try This! Write a sentence telling why a vet might take an x-ray of an animal.

C and E

Name _____

C C C C C

E E E E E

C E

Chris Chris

Ellen Ellen

Ed E. Cat likes eggs.

Try This! Write two names that begin with **C**. Write two names that begin with **E**.

D and L

Name _____

D D D D

L L L L

D L

Deb Deb

Lyle Lyle

Deb likes Lee's dog.

Try This! Write a sentence beginning with **D**. Write another one beginning with **L**.

M and N

Name _____

M M M M M

N N N N N

M N

Mars Mars

Neptune Neptune

Nan met Marsha.

Write a question about Mars or Neptune.

H and K

Name _____

H *H H H H*

K *K K K K*

H *H*

Hank Hank

Kim Kim

Hal K. has kites.

Try This! Write a name beginning with **H** or **K** for each of these animals: hippo, koala, hen, kangaroo.

Q, W, and X

Name _____

Queen Walt Xerox

Try This! Write a sentence using these words: Quebec, Wednesday, Xavier.

Y and Z

Name _____

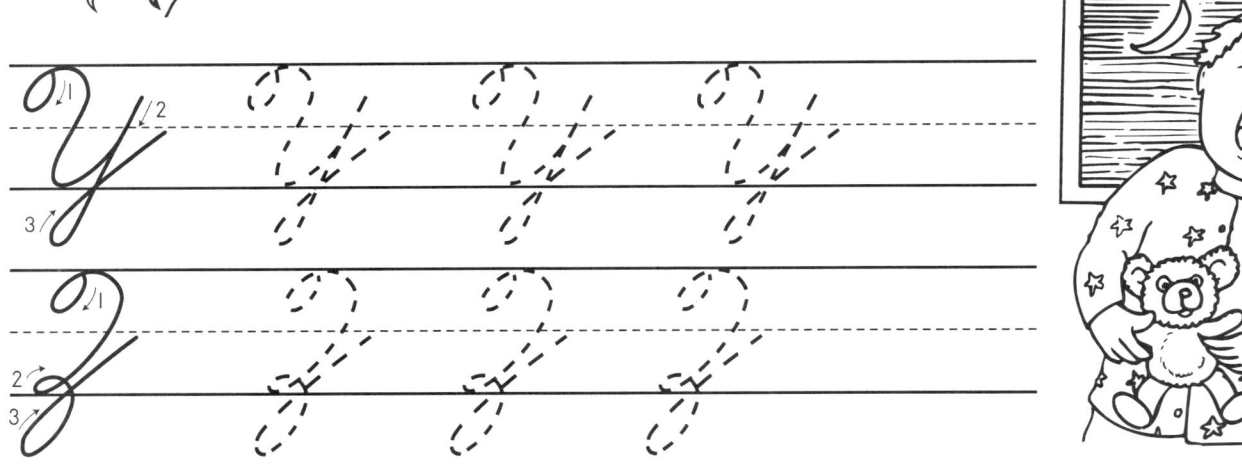

Y   Y   Y   Y

Z   Z   Z   Z

y

Yvette   Yvette

Zach   Zach

Young Zeke yawns.

Try This! Look in a dictionary. Write an interesting word that begins with **Y** and another that begins with **Z**.

F and T

Try This! Write two names that begin with **T**. Write two names that begin with **F**.

G and S

Name _____

G

S

g

Gail

Sid

Sue G. sips soda.

Try This! Look in an atlas. Write three countries that begin with **G**. List three countries that begin with **S**.

B, P, and R

Name _____

B B B B B

P P P P P

R R R R R

B P R

B P R

Bob Pippi Rover

Try This! Write a sentence. See if you can use words beginning with **B**, **P**, and **R**.

Three Cheers for Capitals!

A–Z

Name _____

Write the letters from **A** to **Z**.

Try This!   Write the initials of every member of your family.

Balloon Count

Number words
one to *ten*

Name _____

Write the number words.

- one
- two
- three
- four
- five
- six
- seven
- eight
- nine
- ten

Try This! Write the number word that tells what year it is.

Announcing the Days

Days of the week

Name _____

Write the days of the week.

Sunday

Monday

Tuesday

Wednesday

Thursday

Friday

Saturday

Try This! Look on a calendar. Write what day will be the last day of the year.

Months of the Year

Name _____

Write the months.

January   April   July   October
February   May   August   November
March   June   September   December

Try This! Write what month it will be six months from now.

Countries Around the World

Letter review

Name _____

Copy this list of countries. The list contains every letter of the alphabet.

Haiti	Jamaica	Bolivia
Iraq	Finland	Swaziland
Egypt	Turkey	Mexico

_____
_____
_____
_____
_____
_____
_____

 Write one fact about one of the countries on the list.